YOUR PASSPORT TO

SPAIN

by Douglas Hustad

CONTENT CONSULTANT

Virginia Ruifernández-Conde, PhD
Assistant Professor of Spanish
Michigan State University

CAPSTONE PRESS
a capstone imprint

Capstone Captivate is published by Capstone Press, an imprint of Capstone.
1710 Roe Crest Drive
North Mankato, Minnesota 56003
www.capstonepub.com

Library of Congress Cataloging-in-Publication Data
Names: Hustad, Douglas, author.
Title: Your passport to Spain / Douglas Hustad.
Description: North Mankato : Capstone Press, 2021. | Series: World passport
    | Includes index. | Audience: Grades 4-6
Identifiers: LCCN 2020001024 (print) | LCCN 2020001025 (ebook) | ISBN
    9781496684103 (hardcover) | ISBN 9781496688026 (paperback) | ISBN
    9781496684615 (pdf)
Subjects: LCSH: Spain—Juvenile literature.
Classification: LCC DP17 .H87 2021 (print) | LCC DP17 (ebook) | DDC
    946—dc23
LC record available at https://lccn.loc.gov/2020001024
LC ebook record available at https://lccn.loc.gov/2020001025

Image Credits
iStockphoto: Starcevic, 15; Newscom: Juan Carlos Rojas/picture alliance, 23; Red Line Editorial: 5; Shutterstock Images: AdrianNunez, cover (bottom), Alex Cimbal, 20, Caron Badkin, 21, dimbar76, 14, Iakov Filimonov, 9, 24, karnavalfoto, 6, KikoStock, 28, Loveshop, cover (flag), lunamarina, 19, Migel, 25, Radu Bercan, 17, Robert Biedermann, cover (map), Shelly Wall, 11, Tatiana Bralnina, 18, Ververidis Vasilis, 27, Vladimir Sazonov, 13
Design Elements: iStockphoto, Shutterstock Images

Editorial Credits
Editor: Jamie Hudalla; Designer: Colleen McLaren

Printed in the United States of America.
PA117

CONTENTS

Words in **bold** are in the glossary.

CHAPTER ONE

WELCOME TO SPAIN!

The sun rises over a hill in Granada in southern Spain. The rays of sunshine cast shadows through the arches of the Alhambra. The ancient **fortress** has tall towers. Visitors can get a beautiful view of the city of Granada from these towers.

The Alhambra allows visitors to walk through the history of Spain. The fortress's walls tell stories of its past. They are carved with Arabic letters. The Alhambra once served as a palace for Muslim rulers. It also has palaces built by Christian kings and queens. These are just two of many religious groups that have lived in Spain over the years. The culture of Spain is a mix of these influences.

MAP OF SPAIN

Pamplona ●

Pyrenees Mountains

Segovia ● ▲ Aqueduct of Segovia

Barcelona ●

■ MADRID

SPAIN

Buñol ●

Ibiza

▲ Mosque-Cathedral of Córdoba

Alhambra ▲
● Granada

■ Capital City
● City
⬢ Landform
▲ Landmark

N
W   E
S

Explore Spain's cities and landmarks.

The city of Valencia lies on the coast of the Mediterranean Sea.

THE SPANISH

Spanish is the country's official language. Catalan, Galician, and Basque are official languages in certain regions. Many **ethnic groups** live in Spain. The largest groups come from Romania and Morocco.

FACT FILE

OFFICIAL NAME: .... KINGDOM OF SPAIN
POPULATION: .... 50 MILLION
LAND AREA: .... 192,657 SQ. MI. (498,980 SQ KM)
CAPITAL: .... MADRID
MONEY: .... EURO
GOVERNMENT: .... CONSTITUTIONAL MONARCHY
LANGUAGE: .... SPANISH

GEOGRAPHY: Spain is located in southwestern Europe on the Iberian Peninsula. It borders Portugal and France. The Mediterranean Sea touches its eastern and southeastern coasts. The Atlantic Ocean touches its northwestern coast.

NATURAL RESOURCES: Spain has coal, iron ore, copper, lead, zinc, and uranium.

Spain has made important contributions to the world. Spanish is the second-most-spoken language in the world. Artists such as Pablo Picasso created famous paintings. People enjoy Spanish food and culture all over the globe.

FACT

Spain is the fourth-largest country in Europe. It is 192,657 square miles (498,980 square kilometers). It could fit inside Russia 33 times.

CHAPTER TWO

HISTORY OF SPAIN

Spain's history involves **invasions** and the arrival of many ethnic groups. Phoenicians from near modern-day Lebanon arrived shortly after 800 **BCE**. They settled in the area that is now Spain. In the 200s BCE, the Romans took control of Spain. The Romans ruled the area for 600 years.

SHIFTS IN POWER

Germanic people called Visigoths **conquered** Spain in the 400s **CE**. In the 700s CE, people called Moors from North Africa wanted to spread the religion of Islam around the world. They ruled for 800 years. The Moors introduced paper, musical instruments, and new crops. Native Spaniards, Moors, and Jewish people all lived there until 1492.

FACT
|||||||||||||||||||||||||||||||||||||||||||||||||||||||||

Romans called the area they settled in Hispania. That is where the modern-day name *Spain* comes from.

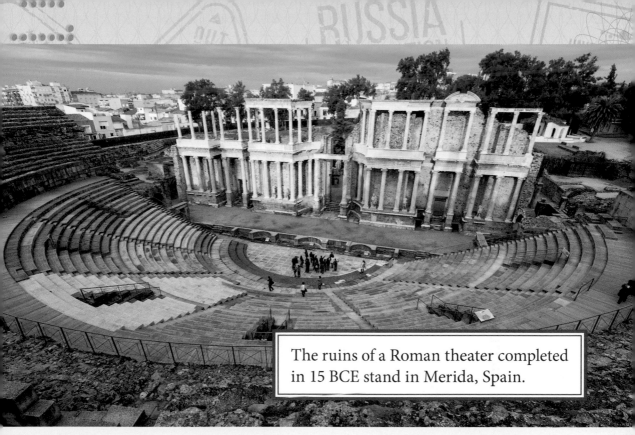

The ruins of a Roman theater completed in 15 BCE stand in Merida, Spain.

Then, Queen Isabella I of Castile became Spain's first queen. She ordered the Jews and Moors to leave the country. She wanted Spain to be a Catholic nation.

THE SPANISH EMPIRE

In 1492, Spain sent explorer Christopher Columbus to the Americas. Spanish soldiers and explorers called **conquistadors** expanded the Spanish **Empire** in the 1500s. It stretched from the Americas to Asia. The conquistadors took much of the native peoples' lands by force.

TIMELINE OF SPANISH HISTORY

700s BCE: Southern Spain is invaded by Mediterranean people called Phoenicians.

228 BCE: Carthaginians from Northern Africa move to southern Spain.

218 BCE: Romans conquer Spain.

400s CE: Germanic people called Visigoths conquer Spain.

711: Moorish Muslims conquer Spain.

1492: Christian kingdoms defeat Muslim rulers.

THE RESULT OF WAR

In the 1800s, France invaded Spain in the Peninsular War (1807–1814). French forces took control of Madrid. The people of Madrid rebelled against the French. The French army killed many of Madrid's people. By 1814, Spain had fought off the French. It regained control of the country.

By 1898, Spain had lost a lot of its colonies. Then the Spanish Civil War began in 1936. Spanish military officers overthrew the **democratic** government. An army led by General Francisco Franco seized power in 1939. Franco led the country as a **dictator**.

Juan Carlos (right) became king of Spain in 1975 and helped form the constitutional monarchy.

Franco died in 1975. Spain returned to a democratic government. Today, Spain has a constitutional monarchy. This means the country has a king. But the **prime minister** leads the government.

MADRID

The city of Madrid was founded in 854 CE. It became the capital in 1561. Today, more than 3 million people live there. It is popular with **tourists** for its many cultural attractions. The Prado National Museum has art from as long ago as the 1100s. The Reina Sofía houses some of the best examples of modern art.

CHAPTER THREE

EXPLORE SPAIN

The Romans influenced Spain in many ways. They built roads and aqueducts. Aqueducts carry water from a source, such as a river, to where people need it. Some of these aqueducts are still standing 2,000 years later.

FACT

Spain has a mix of Islamic and Christian history. An example is in the city of Córdoba. In the 700s CE, ruler 'Abd al-Raḥmān I ordered construction of a mosque. That mosque was made into a Christian cathedral in 1236. It is still used as a cathedral today. It is called the Mosque-Cathedral of Córdoba.

Romans built the Aqueduct of Segovia in the first century CE. It carried water from the Frio River to the city of Segovia. That was a 10-mile (16-kilometer) trip. It has a large stone bridge. The bridge stands more than 93.5 feet (28.5 meters) high. The aqueduct is a symbol of Segovia.

THE SAGRADA FAMILIA

Another Spanish landmark is the Sagrada Familia.
Josep Maria Bocabella decided to build the church in
Barcelona. This church has been a work in progress
since March 19, 1882.

In 1883, Antoni Gaudí took over designing the
church. Gaudí designed a modern-looking church
with tall towers. Work went on slowly for the next 30
years. Gaudí died in 1926. The church was still under
construction. He was buried in what had been built of
the church.

The Sagrada Familia continues to be built as Gaudí had planned.

Someone started a fire in the church in 1936. This was during the Spanish Civil War. Gaudí's original plans and models were destroyed. It took 16 years to put the models back together. As of 2020, the Sagrada Familia was still not completed. The church relies on donations to continue work on it.

IBIZA

Ibiza is an island off the east coast of Spain. It is well known for its music venues. Ibiza is a center for dance music. People from around the world come to experience the Ibiza music scene.

The waters around Ibiza are full of life. More than 220 species of coral live in its reefs. People love to dive in the area's blue water.

People enjoy sitting on Ibiza's beaches and swimming in the Mediterranean Sea.

Ibiza also has pieces of Spanish history. Settlers founded a port on Ibiza in the 600s BCE. Ancient artifacts of civilization await discovery. Visitors can find ancient burial sites, pottery, and more.

SPANISH TOURISM

Spain is the second-most-visited country in the world. The country set a record in 2017. There were 82 million visitors. Most of those tourists were European people. Many visited Spain in the winter to enjoy nice weather. Spain gets more visitors from the United Kingdom than from anywhere else.

CHAPTER FOUR

DAILY LIFE

Life is not all that different in Spain than in other European countries. But the structure of the Spanish day is quite different from many other countries. The main meal in Spain is lunch. Most people eat lunch between 2:00 and 3:00 p.m. Dinner is a lighter meal. It is typically eaten later in the evening, around 9:00 to 10:00 p.m.

Work and school hours follow this schedule. There is a long lunch break in the afternoon. It lasts from 2:00 to 5:00 p.m. Most businesses are closed. People then go back to work or school until around 8:00 p.m.

FOOD

The Spanish day is built around food. Family and friends gather for meals. This is especially true for Sunday lunch. It is a tradition to make the famous Spanish rice-and-meat dish called paella on Sundays.

Some restaurants offer outdoor seating.

Paella can be made with seafood, including mussels.

One style of Spanish eating is perfect for large gatherings. Tapas are small plates of food. A group can order several dishes and share them. Tapas can be eaten any time of day. Sometimes people eat tapas and then go out for a full meal. Most restaurants in Spain offer tapas.

The most common times to have tapas in Spain are between lunch and supper, and after supper.

GAZPACHO

Gazpacho is a cold soup. Spanish people enjoy it in summer. It is a refreshing meal on warm days. With the help of an adult, you can make gazpacho at home!

Gazpacho Ingredients:

- 2 pounds of tomatoes
- 1 small cucumber
- 1 medium green bell pepper
- 1 slice of dry white bread
- ½ of a small red onion
- 2 small cloves of garlic
- 3 tablespoons olive oil
- 2 tablespoons sherry vinegar or red wine vinegar
- ½ teaspoon cumin
- Salt and pepper as needed

Gazpacho Instructions:

1. Combine all ingredients in a blender and blend until smooth.
2. Transfer to a bowl and place in refrigerator for at least four hours.
3. Serve cold with optional toppings such as croutons, fresh herbs, and black pepper.

Some families attend Catholic mass together.

The King Abdul Aziz Mosque in Marbella opened in 1981.

FAMILY

Time with family is important in Spain. It is common for extended families to live together, or at least close by. Children also often live with their parents into adulthood. It is common to take care of older members of the family.

Catholicism remains the most practiced religion in Spain. About 69 percent of the country is Roman Catholic. The second-most-practiced religion is Islam. More than 1 million Muslims live in Spain. That is about 2 percent of the population. There are also many other religions practiced in Spain. Judaism is one of them.

CHAPTER FIVE

HOLIDAYS AND CELEBRATIONS

Every major city in Spain has a yearly festival. La Tomatina happens in August in Buñol. The city is famous for its tomatoes. People throw them at each other in a big food fight.

National Day is October 12. It celebrates the day Christopher Columbus arrived in the Caribbean in 1492. People around the country get the day off from work. There is a military parade in Madrid. It is broadcast around Spain.

RELIGIOUS HOLIDAYS

Many of Spain's major holidays come from Christian traditions. These holidays started as ways to remember important events. They can also honor religious figures.

People get covered in tomatoes during La Tomatina.

The three kings are the three wise men who visited baby Jesus.

Christmas is one of Spain's most important celebrations. Major cities set up markets. People buy food and homemade gifts there. One market in Barcelona dates back to the 1700s. Three Kings Day is January 6. It is the end of the Christmas season. Children write letters to the three wise men found in the Bible. Children ask them for the gifts they want.

RUNNING OF THE BULLS

Many cities in Spain have festivals every year. Pamplona holds its San Fermín Festival every summer. The most famous part of the festival is the Running of the Bulls.

The bulls' sharp horns can easily injure people during the Running of the Bulls in Pamplona.

In the 1800s, people started running alongside bulls as a challenge. The bull run in Pamplona takes place every day for seven days. The bulls are driven from farmland into the city. The run starts at 7:55 a.m. Six bulls are released at the sound of a rocket. The run is less than 1,000 yards (914 m). It lasts only a few minutes. But those minutes are very dangerous. People get seriously injured every year. Fourteen people died between 1924 and 2009. But the challenge of making the famous run keeps people trying each year.

CHAPTER SIX

SPORTS AND RECREATION

Spain's most popular sport is *fútbol*. This is Spanish for "soccer." The country is home to La Liga. This is one of the best professional men's leagues in the world. Also popular is the men's national team. La Roja, Spanish for "The Reds," are known for their playing style. The team relies on quick passes and lots of movement. It used that style to win the country's first World Cup in 2010.

FACT

Barcelona hosted the 1992 Summer Olympics. Spain had its best-ever performance at the Games with 13 gold medals.

Some Spanish people enjoy cycling. Sometimes there are cycling races. Spanish people sometimes go downhill skiing. The Pyrenees Mountains are one popular ski spot.

Lionel Messi started playing for Barcelona in La Liga in 2003.

People typically dance the flamenco to guitar music.

People in Spain also enjoy artistic activities, such as dancing. The flamenco is a famous dance that a variety of Spain's ethnic groups developed. It features lots of arm movement and stomping of the feet.

From the soccer field to the dance floor, there are many activities to do in Spain. The country also offers a variety of beautiful buildings and sites for everyone to see.

CHAPAS

Chapas is an outdoor game. It can be played with 2 to 12 friends. In English, it is called the bottle cap game.

1. Choose a bottle cap.
2. Draw a racecourse on the sidewalk with chalk.
3. Players take turns flicking their bottle cap forward. If it goes outside the lines of the course, that player must start over.
4. The first one to cross the finish line wins.

GLOSSARY

BCE/CE
BCE means Before Common Era, or before year one. CE means Common Era, or after year one

**conquered
(KAHNG-kuhrd)**
took control of an area

**conquistadors
(kon-KEYS-tuh-dors)**
16th century military leaders from Spain

**democratic
(dem-uh-KRAT-ik)**
having to do with a government system in which people vote on the way the country is led

**dictator
(DIK-tay-tuhr)**
a leader who has complete control over a country

empire (EM-pire)
a large area ruled by an emperor

**ethnic groups
(ETH-nik GROOPS)**
people who share a common culture, race, language, or nationality

fortress (FOR-triss)
a building designed for defending itself

**invasions
(in-VEY-zhuhnz)**
when people enter other areas to try to take control of them

**prime minister
(PRIME MIN-uh-stur)**
a head of government

tourists (TOOR-ists)
people who visit another country

READ MORE

City Trails: Barcelona. New York: Lonely Planet Kids, 2018.

Howse, Jennifer. *Spain*. New York: Weigl, 2019.

Rechner, Amy. *Spain*. Minneapolis, MN: Bellwether Media, 2019.

INTERNET SITES

DK Find Out!: Conquistadors
https://www.dkfindout.com/us/history/explorers/conquistadors

National Geographic Kids: Spain Country Profile
https://kids.nationalgeographic.com/explore/countries/spain

National Geographic Kids: Spain Facts
https://www.natgeokids.com/za/discover/geography/countries/spain-facts

INDEX

OTHER BOOKS IN THIS SERIES

YOUR PASSPORT TO CHINA
YOUR PASSPORT TO ECUADOR
YOUR PASSPORT TO EL SALVADOR
YOUR PASSPORT TO ETHIOPIA
YOUR PASSPORT TO FRANCE
YOUR PASSPORT TO IRAN
YOUR PASSPORT TO KENYA
YOUR PASSPORT TO PERU
YOUR PASSPORT TO RUSSIA